SHORT PARAGRAPHS ON LISTENING

Benjamin Mathes

For Allison, who taught me what it feels like to finally be heard.

A Free Listening Movement

Born on the streets of Los Angeles in 2012, Urban Confessional: A Free Listening Movement began as a community of artists determined to offer a compassionate, non-judgmental presence to anyone in need.

Every week, they stood on street corners in LA with signs that said "Free Listening" and opened their hearts to anyone who needed to be heard.

Over the years, the movement has grown to include thousands of volunteers from all walks of life in over 80 countries.

The following short paragraphs were written by the movement's founder, Benjamin Mathes, and are based on lessons learned from the streets.

For more info or to join the movement, please visit: www.urbanconfessional.org

"Aren't human beings so sweet."
--Catherine Fitzmaurice

"Being heard is so close to being loved that most people can't tell the difference."
--David Augsburger

There's a lot to say about listening.

I'll try to keep it brief.

These are in no particular order.

Isn't that fun?

One About Relationships

Relationships would be much easier if there was only one person involved. It seems like the closer we get to people, the more complicated things become and the harder it is to listen. Expectations, emotions, and feelings get involved and make it difficult to stay present and listen to each other. When we stop listening, we start hurting. When we start hurting, relationships stop thriving. Offer your listening to the people closest to you. Your husbands, your wives, partners, and family. Ask them questions, listen to their answers, and give them your attention.

Listening is the quickest path to loving, and love mitigates all risk, even in relationships.

One About Listening With Your Heart

So much can be said without saying anything.

The heart, the breath, and the body have a way of telling a truth our lips are too afraid to tell.

Listen deeply to the deepest parts of yourself and let the heart do the communicating.

One About Listening To People We Don't Like

Today, it seems like it's easy to dislike people who think differently than we do. Groups of people are categorized based on their political preference, cultural tendencies, or religious affiliation. It's easy to mistake the policies of an institution for the complexities of an individual. When we hear things we don't like, we can become angry, reactive, and bitter. We stop listening, and start judging. These judgments divide us, keep us from understanding, and make listening impossible. They keep us from bridging the gaps of disagreement and division.

How do we find unity in our disagreement?

Begin with understanding their story, put yourself in their shoes, and recognize their humanity. We don't have to like everyone, we just need to understand them. It's the quickest path to unity.

One About Wholeness

We are light and dark. We are full and empty. We are up and down. We are whole. When we start to accept our weakness, it becomes the source of understanding we need to accept others' weaknesses.

Believe it or not, deep Listening often guides us into our shared weaknesses and there we discover our shared strengths. It's an experience of growth, of compassion, and of celebration.

One About Fixing Problems

Many of us are fixers. When we notice a problem, we like to fix it. Sometimes, though, we forget to listen and we fix a problem that never existed. In difficult and chaotic times, action is certainly required. But when we act before we listen, we often add to the chaos.

Listening is not a substitute for doing. Listening is the prerequisite for doing.

Listen first, act with purpose, speak with love, and make the world a better place. But don't forget, sometimes we need to shut up and listen before we get up and do.

One About Young People

The future is listening.

One About Bad News

There's a lot of bad news out there. It seems like every day there is tragedy, confusion, and disharmony. We live in a broken world. But, if all we see is the brokenness, we will never heal. We can bring light into dark places, we can show the world something else, we can be a voice for unity and understanding.

You are real.

Joy is real.

Listen.

One About Stealing

There is something we can take that always benefits the people we love. We can take it without asking, without hiding, without stealing. We never have to give it back, and there is always more.

Time.

Take time to be with, to open to, and to love. Take time to ask, to touch, and to allow. Take time to learn from, to laugh with, and to listen to. Take time and give it away. It's the most valuable resource we have, and (believe it or not) it's free.

One About Being With Suffering People

Sometimes, when life seems to be collapsing all around someone we love, we find ourselves wondering what to say, how to be, or what to do. We may feel uncomfortable holding space for someone who is openly suffering or struggling, so we shut down, avoid, and close ourselves off. Or, often, we try to fix, to solve, and to be a hero.

It's a weird thing, but sometimes in these moments of struggle, the most power language is silence. The most healing fix is touch. The most protective action is presence. Words are not always the most effective form of love.

Sometimes there's nothing to say, only someone to be.

One About Ambition

Listening pursues wisdom, not power.

One About Listening When You Don't Want To

There are times when we need to protect ourselves from abuse. Times when discomfort turns to pain, and the need to remove ourselves from a situation is the only healthy choice to make. But, there are also times when discomfort is not abuse and it can shape us. When dissenting beliefs challenge us, and difficult news shakes us. In these times, listening can be unpleasant. It would be much easier to edit out the discomfort, ignore the other side, and live in denial.

But there is a difference between easy and healthy.

Sometimes, the only way out is to go through, and the only way to grow is to have the edges burned a little. The voice of hope speaks most clearly through the fog of discomfort.

The most important time to listen is when you'd rather not.

One About Stories

We are made of stories. We are walking novels whose pages are written everyday. Our stories reflect who we are, who we were, and who we are becoming. And, like roots of a tree, our stories are entirely unique, yet connect us all.

But, unless someone is willing to listen to our story, our story never realizes its full potential.

When no one listens, we can feel that our stories don't matter and, if we're not careful, we can believe that we don't matter. Share your story, listen to others, repeat.

All it will do is change the world.

One About Forgiveness

We can do terrible things to each other. The people we trust can lie to us, the people we need can neglect us, and the ones we love can betray us. But, no matter the depth of the hurt, we have to remember that destruction cannot mend destruction.

Forgiveness doesn't always feel good, but it always is good. Keep listening, keep searching, and keep serving. Don't stop loving the ones around you. It's not over yet.

Don't let their worst stop your best.

One About Inspiration

The voice of inspiration will never yell over the crowd. It will never fight against your distractions, your technology, or the other voices in your head. The voice of inspiration speaks in a gentle whisper, quietly reminding you that you matter, you belong, and you are valued. It whispers a life that ushers you into the future.

Find quiet, find stillness, find solitude, and listen.

One About Borders

There are no government borders, religious differences, or cultural divides in our hearts. People all over the world want the same thing: to be loved, to be valued, and to be heard.

Listen for the longings of their heart, even when, especially when, it's hard to hear.

One About Listening In A New Way

Sometimes the voice we need the most is speaking a language that's hard to hear.

Maybe the voice we need to hear is in a subtle feeling, a gentle reminder, or a whisper from the heart. Maybe it's a loving touch, or a strong embrace, or a home cooked meal. Maybe it's in the little gestures: the held door, the made bed, and the warm coffee.

Sometimes the things we need to hear can only be heard when we find a new way to listen.

One About Listening When Your World Is Upside Down

Listening is the heart's way of being available to the world. When the world is spinning out of control, and we can't seem to find our feet, listening is the moment of calm where clarity is possible because surrender is inevitable.

In tragedy, listen.
In panic, listen.
In confusion, listen.

When everything around you is telling you to shut down, open the ears of your heart, and listen.

One About Listening To Yourself

As we find ourselves in a world of opposing voices, it's important that your listening includes your own voice. You may not always like what you have to say, but it's important to listen.

If your listening does not include yourself, it is incomplete.

One About Being Offended

As we grow in our understanding and acceptance of people, we may experience some growing pains. New ideas, new identities, and new ideologies can create messy conversations. The path to greater acceptance is paved with hurt feelings, offended sensibilities, and difficult conversations. In times of cultural growth, traditional viewpoints are often challenged and you may find yourself frequently offended by those pushing change or by those resisting it.

Cultural growing pains hurt less when we listen.

So, when you're offended, don't end communication too quickly. Don't leave a conversation making assumptions about the other person. Stay. Listen. Ask questions. If someone offends you, seek clarity before you seek conclusions. Did they mean to say what you heard? How did they arrive at this position? Are they open to discuss it further? Maybe there is more to them than their opinion. As we all grow in our own imperfect ways, remember to listen, be patient, and hear the person beneath the opinion.

One About Being Alive

Being heard is a universal need. Deep in all of us is the need to be acknowledged, understood, and loved. When we offer attention without expectation of return, we deepen our understanding of what it means to be alive.

One About Changing Minds

Destructive beliefs and opinions can lead to destructive behavior. Sometimes, the impulse to change someone's mind is healthy and courageous.

But destructive beliefs are often protecting wounded hearts.

If we take the time to hear their hearts, we may get the chance to change their minds. It's a start. It's a jumping off place.

And it's hard.

One About Fathers

To the men who used their strength to serve, their influence to inspire, and their love to empower, we honor you. To the fathers who are always there, always available, and always by our side, we see you. To the fathers who always answer the phone, always answer the call, and always show up, we celebrate you. To the fathers who offer a shoulder, a kick in the butt, and a bad dad-joke, we thank you.

But, most of all, to the fathers who listen, who hold space, and use their strength to understand, we love you.

One About Listening To Others

We have work to do. We have love to share. We have people to hear. When we listen, we allow others to influence us, inspire us, and teach us. When we allow others to speak, we give them the space to be themselves, to express freely, and to feel valued.

This is a good thing.

One About Oneness

True diversity can be celebrated best when we recognize that we are already one. Across the world, people share the need to be loved, accepted, and heard. Perhaps, these needs are the truest thread connecting our common humanity.

We are already together.

We are already one.

One That Tells You What To Do

The world is moving quickly. The world is noisy. The world is asking to be heard. Take time to slow down, open up, and listen. It's free, it's restorative, and it's needed.

Another One About Fixing

I'm guilty. I like to fix things. If you tell me
something's wrong, I go into solution mode. I know
I'm not the only one who does this.

Sometimes, though, all we need to do is listen. All we
need to do is be with the person and let them speak.
They may not need a fix, they may need an ear.

Stop fixing, start listening.

One About Loneliness

The heart of listening is relationship. When we listen, we allow others to influence us, to change us, or to affect us. Listening offers other people the possibility of love and influence in their life. That is the nature of relationship.

Listening conquers loneliness.

—

One About Connection

Today, before you connect digitally, before you find out what happening with people across the world, find out what's happening with people in your world. Talk to your friends, listen to your parents, say hello to the stranger next to you. Tell someone you love them, tell someone you miss them, tell someone you're thinking about them.

When we connect with others, we open up the possibility of relationship and growth.

You may learn something, you may heal something, or you may fall in love.

Connect with someone today.

One About Being Ok

You don't have to be "fine". You don't have to put on a face. You don't have to be strong. You don't have to be who you think we want you to be.

Life is not a static experience.

Sometimes it hurts. Sometimes it's confusing. Sometimes it feels like it's never going to change. Keep going. Keep going. Keep going.

The world needs what you have to give.

There is still love to give. There is still love to receive.

If you feel like you're at the end, raise your hand, ask for help, and know that it's ok to not be ok.

One About Listening To Opinions

There is less distance between hearts than between minds. When we listen, we become available to the heart of the other person. Don't be seduced into an argument with their mind. Instead, revel in the beauty of their heart.

In disagreement, if we can hear their story, their experience, and their struggle we become connected in a way that allows us to hear their humanity. This is how we will navigate through these very difficult times.

Hear the person, not just the opinion.

One About Change

It seems we are united in our desire for change. But before we can change the world, we must hear the world. Unless we listen carefully, we may spend our time trying to change the wrong things.

Before you speak, listen.
Before you respond, listen.
Before you do, listen.

Change begins with listening.

One About Our Blemishes

Too many of us live in a world where we feel evaluated. We struggle to get things right, to be perfect, and to impress. Listening asks that we let go of being perfect, that we accept our blemishes, and love in spite of ourselves.

It's when we accept our own imperfections that we are able to listen to the imperfections of others.

Let listening bring you into greater acceptance of all people.

One About Reflecting

There's a lot of traffic in our lives, and if we're not careful, we'll miss the beauty all around us. In order to remain aware and present, we need to establish disciplines of stillness and quiet.

This is the only way to hear the depths of our humanity and to unify ourselves with the world around us.

To hear the world, be available to the world.

One About Healing

Being heard is the first step towards being healed.

Never underestimate the healing power of your attention, your presence, and your care. Be with people, sit in the silence, and listen.

All it will do is change their life.

One About Division

There's a lot going on, and we are more divided than ever before. It seems everyone has something to say, and somewhere to say it. Free speech is beautiful and disagreement is necessary, but it loses its power when it's not received.

When we listen, we open to the possibility of hearing a person, not just an opinion. We make ourselves available to the things that unite us, and to the humanity under the opinion. Through listening, we can find unity in our disagreement.

We don't have to agree with each other to be with each other.

One About Voices

The world outside of us is loud. There are many voices, many opinions, and everyone can speak their mind. But the world inside of us can be even louder. Pain, anger, and hurt can be so loud that sometimes it's all we can hear.

Even so, listen closely.

Behind every voice of pain is a gentle voice of hope whispering for your attention. Behind every voice of hurt, is the sound of redemption and healing.

The truth is often a whisper.

Listen carefully, the loudest voice isn't always the truth.

One About Hearts & Minds

Disagreement can create distance between people. If we don't work to bridge that distance, we stay divided and in conflict. We begin to see the world as "us and them", we protect ourselves from different opinions and different people, and the distance between us grows bigger.

We allow our minds to separate our hearts.

But, we are more than our opinions. We all have hopes and fears. We all love someone or want to love someone or used to love someone. We all have been hurt, are healing, or trying to heal.

Our minds may disagree, but our hearts understand.

Listen with your heart, listen to their heart, and discover that there is less distance between hearts than between minds.

One About Attention

There is nothing more valuable than the gift of our attention. Too often, we impose our intention on other people. We want to change their mind, win the argument, or tell our side of the story. We stop asking questions, stop being curious, and stop listening.

But when we give our attention, we create a space where others feel free to speak and are open to listen.

Attention never demands, attention never judges, attention never fights to be right. Attention is a pure offering of our heart's interest. To truly listen, quickly surrender your intention, and freely offer your attention.

One About Moms

When we give our mothers the gift of our attention, we receive the gift of their wisdom.

Ask them questions, listen to their response, and remember where you came from. A mother's strength comes from many places, but the strength of their wisdom is only received when we listen.

Honor those who brought you into this world, and honor those who teach you how to navigate through it.

To those who are mothers, who want to be mothers, and those who use their strength to mother the ones who are lost, we honor you, we thank you, and we are listening.

Listen to your mother.

One About Listening 'til The End

Too many people stop listening once they've heard enough to form a response. They stop listening too soon. What if we're patient? What if we allow the person to finish before we respond? What if we seek to understand, not to correct? When we listen until the end, we allow ourselves the possibility of meaningful conversation, deepening relationship, and genuine connection. Be patient, be open, and listen until the end.

One About Giving

There is a joy that only the generous can discover.
A joy that renews, a joy that replenishes, and a joy
that multiplies.

Giving is the only non-possessive form of love.

It is generative and always brings people together.
Giving makes you wealthy, opens your heart, and
heals the world.

One About Community

The nature of community can be complicated. Community, like all relationships, requires we give up control, we make ourselves available, and we open up to the possibility that we may get hurt.

I know, it's a risky place to be.

But, when a group of people are united and working for a common cause, their power is undeniable. Work hard to believe in the people around you, invest in them, celebrate them, and listen to them. A healthy community is not one void of conflict, it's one that uses conflict to sharpen their belief in each other.

Don't forget, we can do more together than we can alone.

One About Availability

Anywhere.

Anytime.

With Anyone.

Listen.

One About Our Alikeness

It seems like there are plenty of things in this world that can divide us. If we look hard enough, we can always find differences, always find opposition, and always find disagreement. It's easy to do.

But, easy isn't always right.

It might be hard to believe, but there are powers stronger than our differences; there is still goodness between us. We all want to be loved, want to be heard, and want to be valued. We all know the depths of pain and the heights of joy. We've all been confused, been lost, and stumbled across clarity.

We're all in this together.

One About Serving Togetherness

When two people serve together, they grow together, they listen together, and they share an experience that will forever bond them. Serving with another person is a beautiful reminder of the power of community and the joy of togetherness.

One About Risk

If you love them, let them know. If you miss them, let them know. If you've been thinking about them, let them know. If you respect them, let them know. If you admire them, let them know. If they hurt you, let them know. If they raised you up, let them know.

Give them something true to hear.

Risk being known.

Risk relationship.

One About Loving the Hateful

There is only one way to stop the cycle of hate.

There is only one way to end the seductive forces of violence and intolerance.

There is only one way to resist: Love anyway.

As difficult as it is to do, it is a tactic that has been passed down to us for centuries. Without it, the anger will continue, the fighting will escalate, and humanity will suffer.

What does love look like in moments of deep dissention?

Love looks like Listening.

Listening is the quickest way to humanize those who dehumanize others. Get on the front lines of empathy and listen to those who do not listen to you.

It's the only way to break the cycle.

One About the Mystery of Life

You never know what will happen when you make yourself available to others. In this way, listening asks you to let go of controlling the moment. You never know what will happen. Like all forms of love, when you listen you enter into the great mystery of life: the beauty of a shared, spontaneous, and meaningful experience with another person.

One About Changing Humanity

If we want humanity to become something it's never
become, we're going to have to do something
we've never done. Something we're not good at,
something messy, something difficult. Like it or not,
the responsibility to change the world lies with those
not yet blinded by it.

We must listen to the ones we don't want to listen to.

We must love the ones we don't want to love.

They are hurting, and we need to hear their hurt if we
want to end their hate.

One About Worthiness

Loving others begins with remembering that you are loved and worthy, and loved and worthy and loved and worthy and loved and worthy and loved and worthy and loved and worthy and loved and worthy and loved and worthy and loved and worthy.

All the time.

One About Noise

Our minds are loud. In fact, it may be safe to say that most of the noise in the world comes from our minds. Sometimes when things are loud, we close our ears. But sometimes things are loud because they're in pain and they don't know what else to do.

Pay attention, step into the noise, ask for help, and listen it back to clarity.

One About Love When It Sucks

They forgot to call. They said something hurtful. They disagreed with you. They're always late. They never listen. They dishonored you. They left you when you needed them most.

Love them anyway.

One About Being Depressed

Sometimes, when it feels like the world is collapsing around us,
when it's hard to keep going, and it seems like no one cares, there is a small voice whispering, "It's ok, you're ok."

This voice may be a friend, a lyric in a song, or a stranger with a sign. If you listen closely enough, you will hear the voice you so desperately need. It may be hard right now, and the darkness may seem endless, but keep going. Listen deeply.

Hope is real, love is waiting, and someone is listening.

One About What You (Really) Need

To be a good listener, you do not need a degree.
You do not need an ordination. You do not need
permission. You do not need to be anyone other than
who you are.

All you need is what you already have.

One About Being Loved

When you're lost, you are loved. When you're hurt, you are loved. When you're at fault, you are loved. When you win, you are loved. When you lose, you are loved. When it seems like everything is collapsing around you, you are still loved.

This applies to everyone, and precedes listening.

You are always loved.

One About Hope

I know it's loud out there. There's a lot of bad news, and it seems like every day brings new opportunities to lose hope. But, I promise, there is a quiet army of people working to bring hope into the world.

People creating movements, nursing others to health, and bringing light into dark places. Organizations and projects that maybe you've never heard of are fighting on behalf of hope.

Hope is not lost.
Hope is not fading.
Hope is real.
Hope is happening.

One About Signs

We hold many signs. Some of us carry signs that push people away, or signs that bring people in. Some of us carry signs from our past, and hold them up like it's our present. We bear signs of love, signs of trauma, and signs of healing. No matter the sign, it's ok to hold it, it's ok to show it, and it's ok to let others see it.

It's also ok to drop your signs and replace them with new ones.

It's not easy, and it takes work, but, it's possible to replace a sign of pain with a sign of healing. It's possible to drop a sign of fear and replace it with a sign of joy.

It's a long journey, and you can't do it alone.

What sign are you holding?
What sign are you ready to drop?

One About Being Asked To Leave

One day, Craig and a friend were Free Listening outside of Trinity College in Dublin, Ireland. Suddenly, they were asked to leave because an academic complained about their presence.

There will always be people encouraging you not to listen.

In the face of great pressure, it's still important to stay present, to listen, and gently usher people into acceptance with compassion.

One About Listening in Disagreement

Everyone has something to say and somewhere to say it. With all this talk, we're going to disagree sometimes. When we do, work hard to hear the person behind the opinion.

Get their story, hear their heart, and ask, "How did you arrive at this opinion?"

When we get the biography not just the ideology, we can learn to hear the person not just the opinion.

One About Strength

We are meant to experience life, and sometimes
that means we have to allow ourselves to experience
"unpleasant" emotions.

It's ok.

Strength comes from our ability to be open,
to feel fully, to listen deeply, and to allow.

One About the Rain

There are times when the rain seems unending, and floods seem inevitable. This is when listening matters most. When all seems lost and conditions seem overwhelming.

Listen anyway.

An open ear and a willing heart
might be the only umbrella you ever need.

One About Duty

Loving others begins with giving them your attention, your presence, and your listening. It requires an offering of the entire self, and is a complete form of loving.

It is, indeed, the first duty of love.

One About What We Need More Of

We need more people whose influence never outreaches their compassion and whose generosity is boundless. People who listen before they respond, who understand before they move forward, and who are patient in conflict. Who value being with over being right. Who see beneath the surface. Who stay in it with you. Who stand beside you. Who will pick you back up, back up, back up, and back up again. Who never need to know more than they are willing to experience. Who see and believe in the grey area. Who still love you when it's hard, and hope when it feels impossible. Who can hold an empty space.

We need more people who listen.

One About What Moves Us Forward

The temptation to avoid genuine conversations is powerful. When we open ourselves to honest interactions with another person, we become vulnerable and available to be effected. This can be scary. This vulnerability makes us available to be offended, to be challenged, or to be upset. So, we avoid it, we defend against it, and we hide.

But, the same vulnerability that allows us to be hurt, allows us to be inspired. When we open to another person, we open to the possibility of becoming more than we ever imagined we could become.

Avoidance will keep us in the same place.

Only open, genuine availability to others will move us forward.

One About Freedom

Her: Tomorrow I turn 15, and guess what I'm celebrating?

What are you celebrating?

Her: 75 days free!

75 days free from what?

Her: 75 days free from cutting myself.

…

Listen, and you may hear what freedom sounds like.

One About Others

Our world is moving fast, and many people are traveling alone. We fly by each other and rarely take the time to relate, to connect, or to listen. We end up locked in the vacuum of our own thoughts, isolated in our mind, and alone in a crowded world.

The surest way to step outside the echo chamber of your own thoughts is to listen to other people.

Be open to being affected by different thoughts, experiences, and feelings. It is only when we are open to listening to others that we open ourselves to the differences that make us human. When we listen to other people, we learn something new, love someone new, and grow in ways only the curious will ever grow.

Today, remind yourself to do one simple thing: listen to other people.

One About Connecting

Listen to connect, not to correct.

One About Simplicity

Listening is little. Listening is small. Listening is quiet.

There are no parades, no banners, no awards.

There are no ceremonies, no rewards, no medals.

There is only love.

No gesture of love is too small
to counter the noise of life.

One About Communication

Miscommunication can lead to damaged relationships. When we don't communicate well, we don't feel heard, and we become defensive. Emotions begin to get the better of us, and we say things we don't mean, and hurt people we love.

The art of communication begins with listening, and continues by considering what the other person is hearing.

When we hear with their ears, from their perspective, we speak to the person they are, not the person we believe them to be. This is one way to speak with empathy and compassion so difficult truths can be delivered with love, and relationships can grow.

In the end, what they hear is always more important than what you said.

One About Always

When it's tough to hear, listen.
When it's loud, listen.
When it's silent, listen.
When all seems lost and you don't know where to go,
listen.
When time is running out, listen.
When everything is beautiful, listen.
When the path is well lit, listen.
When the pain is finally going away, listen.

Always listen.

One About Transformation

True listening goes beyond the function of communication. Listening is not just a transactional event. Listening is not just something you do to get what you want.

True listening is a transformational experience.

It takes us into a deep communion with another person. And, it's in this communion we realize the fullness of our humanity, the oneness of our individuality, and the true nature of our hearts.

One About Brokenness

What if there's nothing to fix.

Maybe our broken pieces are the places where we listen best, the places where the story gets in. The places where we truly understand each other. The places where we are the same. The places that don't need to be perfect, don't need to be right, don't need to be better–than.

Maybe if my brokenness could talk to your brokenness it would say this:

"But, I'm all broken."

And maybe if your brokenness was listening to my brokenness it would say this:

"Yea, me too."

Then, we could finally be together.

One About Perfect Listening

Perfect listening includes imperfect listening.

Like perfect nature includes imperfect things.

Who can find the perfect tree? Or leaf? Or cloud?

Wholeness includes brokenness.

Listening includes distraction.

And "I" includes "you."

One About the Politics Of It All

These are significant times for the United States. For some, this is a time of hope and excitement. For others, this is a time filled with fear and uncertainty. People may celebrate, cheer, march, and smile. And still, we must listen. People may offend us, hurt us, challenge us, or ignore us. And still, we must listen.

We must listen.

One About Hustle

In the hustle, in the hurry, in the rush, it can be hard
to listen.

But, this is when it's needed the most.

If you feel life is moving too quickly, pause and listen.
Take in the world around you and be grateful.

You might discover that time is not moving quickly,
you are.

One About Truth

Truth is a tricky thing.

Have you ever met someone who uses truth to damage other people. Who justifies relational destruction by saying, "I'm just telling the truth."

Truth is necessary, beautiful, and real, but it must never outrun love.

Love must outrun truth.

One About the Many Faces Of Love

Love takes many shapes and has many names. Love in time looks like patience, love in conflict looks like compassion, and love in plenty looks like joy.

When we listen, we open ourselves to experience the many shapes and names of love. We also, in turn, offer that love to the person we're listening to.

There is no distance between listening and loving. It is a direct path with no barriers.

One About Hiding Stories

We all have stories. Stories that shape our lives and remind us of who we are. If these stories are not told, if no one listens to them, we might believe they aren't worth sharing… that WE aren't worth sharing.

Don't hold it in.

Tell someone your story. Ask them to listen. Your story is beautiful, unique, and shapes the person you are. Tell a friend, tell a stranger, or tell your family.

Just don't leave it inside.

One About Opinions

How boring the world would be if we all thought the same way. Some of us are lucky to live in a dynamic society where thought is diverse and opinions are free. We can challenge, change, and argue for and against our beliefs. Sometimes, however, things get personal, and we confuse an opinion with a person. Then we start to treat people based on our opinion of their opinion: "If I like what you think, I'll like who you are."

This has made us more divided.

We can oppose opinions, oppose thought, oppose belief, and not oppose the person who has the belief. Stand for opinions, stand for beliefs, stand for thought, but first, stand for people.

One About Facebook

Our Facebook feeds are littered with articles, posts, and images from all types of people. For some of us, this is difficult to handle, so we edit out the ones we disagree with until our feed looks more like an echo board of our own thoughts.

If we're not careful, we'll treat people this way. Editing out the ones we disagree with until we're surrounded by people who are just like us. Then wonder why we're so divided.

Life is not a Facebook feed.

One About History and Forgiving

We listen through the filter of our history. What we hear is informed by our experiences of the other person.

If your shared past is a place of joy and love, you will listen through the lens of compassion and acceptance. If your shared past is one of conflict and trauma, you will listen with defensiveness, often hearing echoes of a difficult past.

Forgiveness allows us to wash the lens, change the filter, and hear the person as they are today, not as we remember from yesterday. Forgiveness and listening are inseparable acts. If we cannot forgive a past, we cannot hear a present.

One About Closeness

It's easy to distance ourselves from one another. It's easy to turn a blind eye. It's easy to create "us" and "them".

It's easy. But it's not better.

Listening brings us into closeness with one another. It lessens the distance and provides the opportunity for deep understanding.

We need more of that right now.

One About Hard Times

Survivors of trauma often struggle to share their stories and wrestle with the very real, personal, and, often, private effects of trauma.

These are delicate and important stories.

I wish we had answers. I wish it could be another way. I wish the world was different. But, in difficult times, there is hope. There is light. There are people who stand for love. Who lead with compassion. Who listen without limit. There are people whose kindness covers the darkness like a shield. There are people.

Your trauma is real.
Your memories are true.

And, still, there is hope.

One About Each of Us

Each of us is a story. Each of us knows as much about ourselves as others know about themselves.

We all know joy, and fear, and messing up, and loving, and being embarrassed, and feeling guilty, and we all have birthdays.

We all love someone, and have someone who loves us. We've all been scared and nervous and excited. We've been hurt, and have hurt, and have been forgiven, and forgave.

We all have a favorite teacher whose name we still remember. We all remember the first person we fell in love with.

There is unity in our stories. There is unity in our journey. There is unity in us.

Don't give up.
Don't give up.
Don't give up.

One About Sacred Stories

The story of our life is a sacred text written in smiles, hugs, and tears. It is a constantly changing narrative with a few consistent themes: you are worthy, you are loved, and you are worth listening to.

When we open our hearts and listen closely, we discover that everyone is writing their own story, and it's as detailed, troubled, and victorious as our own.

Maybe that's where we'll find our healing; in the realization that we are all writing a story that is both personal and universal, joyous and terrifying, difficult and free.

In short, we are all writing a story that is sacred.

One About a Perspective on Our Differences

Our differences are like puzzle pieces. Each of us shaped uniquely by experience, memories, culture, family, geography to create a perfectly designed piece of the human puzzle. Our opinions and beliefs mold the edges and texture the curved circumference that fit perfectly with other pieces. If we listen closely, if we honor differences, we will see that they can create the places where we fit together.

One for The New Year

Resolutions come and go. Resolutions are forgotten and reset. Resolutions are cliche and uninspired. The world doesn't need another resolution.

The world needs a revolution.

A revolution of love. A revolution of compassion. A revolution of listening. A revolution that begins with you, and changes the world.

Revolution > Resolution

One About Not Knowing

You never know what someone might need. A hug.
A word. A soft place to lay their burdens for a few
minutes. You never know.

The beauty of life's mysteries is only discovered when
we are available, when we are open, when we are
listening.

You never know what someone needs, but if you
listen closely they may just tell you.

One About Winter Holidays

Evolving from ancient practices and solstice rituals, Christmas and other winter holidays are a beautiful reminder that even in our darkest and coldest season, light can be born. That perhaps, hope arrives most completely when we think it has been lost entirely. For many this is a time for hope, joy, love, and peace. But for countless others, this is a season of loneliness.

No matter your perspective on the holidays, let that time of year and the observance of these traditions be a gentle reminder that light often arrives when we expect it least.

You may be by yourself during the holiday season, but you are not alone; there is solidarity even in loneliness.

The holiday season is full of hope, and listening, light and love, even in the darkness of our winter.

One About the Divine

The Divine will never yell at you.

The only way to hear the whisper of the Divine is to listen.

One About Truth

We can only give what we have; only create what we imagine; only change what we first embody.

To receive, give.
To find peace, be peaceful.

To be heard, listen.

One About Some Deep Stuff

When the storm is raging outside of us, it's often a reflection of the storm raging inside of us. Hurt people hurt people. Broken people break people. And when we stop listening to ourselves, we stop listening to others.

Before the world outside you can be heard, you must listen to the word inside you. There may be voices of fear, anxiety, hope, or joy. Remembered pains hiding in shadows that have never truly been heard. Voices from within that have never really been heard. And, just like listening to someone you disagree with, you don't need to believe them to honor their presence and hold space for what they have to say.

It's by honoring every voice inside us that we learn the power of inner discernment, the beauty of self -compassion, and the love of quiet kindness.

The world outside you will never feel heard if the world inside you is still begging for your attention.

One About Hearing Wisdom

Speaking will not calm the chaos, expert analysis will never ease the tension, and social media arguments will never heal relationships.

Listening is wisdom in action, and will carry us through the storm and guide us towards higher ground.

So, when all seems too chaotic, seek the stability that listening offers, and hear the voice of wisdom navigating you through the storm.

One About a Reminder You Need

There are people who will listen. There are people who can hold space for you. There are people who do not judge, or condemn, or belittle. There are people who believe we can heal the things we cannot cure. There are people who will see your heart, honor it, and tell you, "It's ok to not be ok."

There are people who listen.

One About How Sweet Listening Is

Listening guides us into relationship with others, and in doing so, it never forces, never imposes its will, and never demands.

It's a pure offering of attention, presence, and humanity that allows space for agreement and disagreement, harmony and dissent, joy and sorrow.

Listening allows room for paradox and allows us to live in the complexities of the human experience. Sometimes it doesn't make sense. Sometimes it doesn't feel "realistic". Sometimes it doesn't feel effective.

But it is... and that's why it's beautiful.

One About Listening in Tragedy

Some things make no sense. Some pain is too deep to comprehend. Some questions are too big to be answered. And it's in these times that "listening" seems insignificant. Like, "listening" isn't enough, or like "listening" is just a buzz word we use to blanket the profound grief so many are feeling.

I'll be honest, I struggle with this.

But, maybe this is when listening matters most. Maybe listening to the stories of the victims, will help them live forever. Maybe if we listen to the cries of the injured, we can hear the suffering of the world. Maybe by listening to the grief in our hearts, we honor those who are lost. Maybe if we listen to the survivors, we can stand for what's right.

I don't know.

Maybe listening is the truest response.

Maybe.

One About What Listening Won't Do

Listening will not protect you from the shadow.
Listening will not keep you safe. Listening will not
hide you from the darkness of the world.

Listening is not a gentle teacher.

Instead, listening will usher you into the fullness of
the human experience. The light, the shadow, the
pain, the joy, the strength, the weakness—all of it.

Listening will ask you to hear difficult things, to love
the unlovable, to wrestle with the unheard parts of
yourself. And in doing so, listening becomes the
pathway to wholeness, which is the condition of truth.

It's not always pleasant, it's not always clean;
but, it's always there.

One About Endings

Not everything is as it seems. An end can be a beginning, a failure can be a gift, a fall can be a step in the right direction, and a wound can be an opening for love and light.

But, in the middle of life's battles, when the wounds are still fresh, this is hard to believe and difficult to remember.

Sometimes it can feel like the wound is the truth and the source of our identity. I know. I know. I know. But the wound can also be place from which the greatest voice of love is trying to reach you. Stay there. Breathe. And let the light work its way to the center.

There you might learn you are loved, you are worthy, and the wound was a sign of your strength, not a reminder of your weakness.

One About the Author

He lives in Los Angeles. He plays Ultimate Frisbee.
He pee'd in Times Square during the black out
of 2003. He's still rollin with Jesus. He still cries
when Forrest is standing over Jenny's grave. He
loves his wife, a lot. The people in his life are
the most creative, driven, and compassionate people
he knows. He's usually crying on the inside because
it's all so beautiful. He can quote most of "History of
the World, Part 1" and the "Kings of Comedy". He's
always a little homesick. He prefers the mountains
over the beach, unless he's at the beach. He was 5
years old the first time he fell in love.

He is the founder of Urban Confessional: A Free
Listening Movement.

He truly believes listening will make it all better.